A Positive Mind

IS A CONFIDENT MIND

21-Day Journal

Feel Confident Pursuing Your Goals

Coach Terri Terrell

COPYRIGHT

A POSITIVE MIND IS A
CONFIDENT MIND
Copyright ©2021 by
Terri Terrell

ALL RIGHTS RESERVED

Printed in the United States of America

21 Days of Positive Thinking to a more Confident You

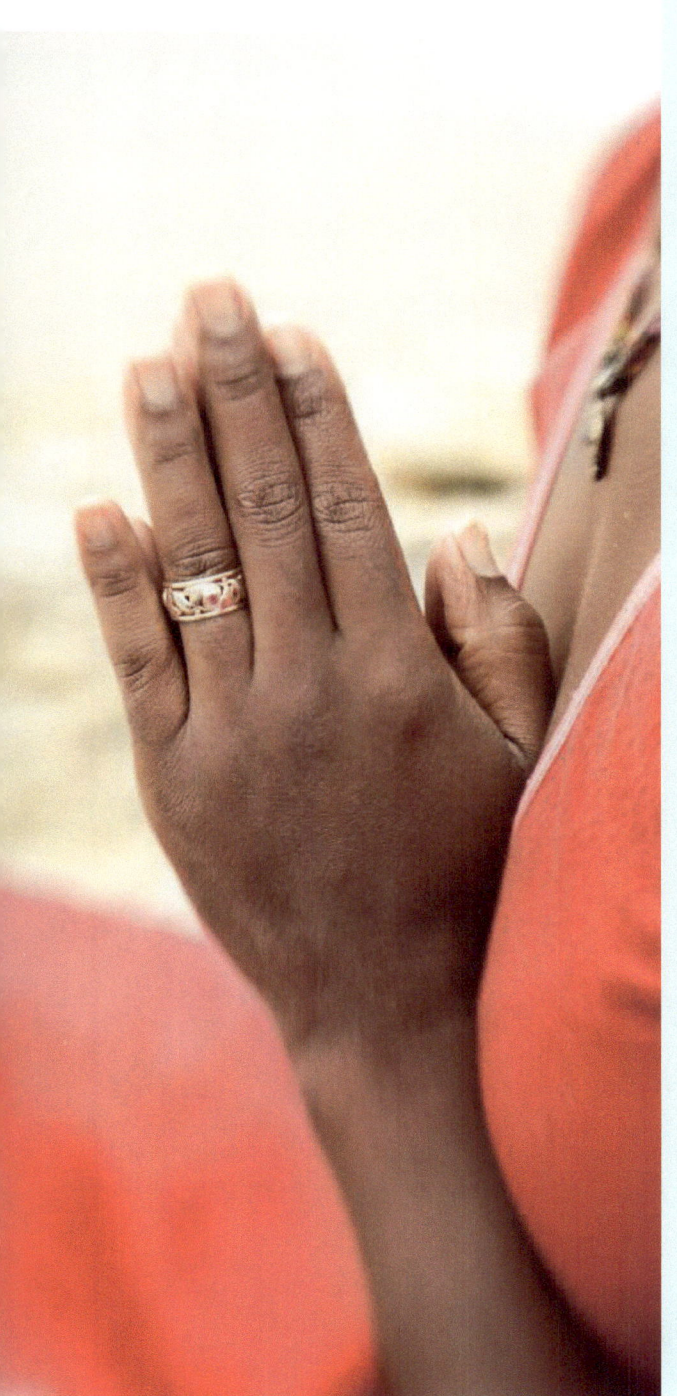

Greetings to your powerful mind,

Thank you for trusting me to be part of your journey towards positive thinking.

Awareness is the first step to healing and change. For these 21 days, you will step into a world of self-awareness, mindset shifts and transformation.

Be prepared to question your limiting beliefs, evaluate your relationships and change the way you think.

My hope is that you will practice positive affirmations and biblical declarations and feel more confident of yourself as time passes.

Here's to a more positive and courageous You.

Sincerely,

Coach Terri

Terri Terrell

Transform your mindset with 1 prompt a day

DAY #1:
Imagine your perfect day. What will you be doing? Where will you be? Whom will you be with?

DAY #2:
What is one thing you are happy and grateful for, today? Why are you grateful and happy about it?

DAY #3:
Write 10 activities which energize you and make you come 'alive'.

DAY #4:
What are 3 things you can do better than many people out there? If you can come up with more than 3, that's great! (Eg: writing, speaking in front of the camera, dressing up etc)

DAY #5:
What is one good habit you can start which will impact your life? Why would you want to start this habit?

DAY #6:
What is one thing/experience which gave you joy recently? What does this tell you about yourself?

DAY #7:
What is one lesson you've learnt in life which you are grateful for?

DAY #8:
Imagine your perfect room or your 'happy place'. What does it look like? What views does it have? What furniture and items will be in it? What colour scheme will it have?

DAY #9:
What are you looking forward to in the next couple of months? Why does this activity make you happy?

DAY #10:
What is your most favourite quote? Why does it inspire or uplift you?

Terri Terrell

DAY #11:

What is one work or business-related opportunity which you are grateful for? (If you are not working, you can write about one opportunity in life which you are happy to have)

DAY #12:

Write down some of the things you love about your work, your office or your business. (If you are not working, you can write down the things you love about your everyday life)

DAY #13:

What is one thing you want to improve in your life? What specific actions can you take, specific people to meet and specific things you can learn (or do) to achieve this?

DAY #14:

Who are the people you are grateful to have in your life? Name them one by one. Write why you are grateful to have each of them in your life.

DAY #15:

Name a teacher, mentor or coach whom you are grateful for. Why are you grateful for 'knowing' him or her? (You don't have to know them personally. You can be grateful to 'know' or be acquainted with *Coach Kimberly Springer'* work, for example)

DAY #16:

What are the things you have which may cause other people to think: "Man, I wish I had THAT in my life"?

Terri Terrell

DAY #17:

What are you proud of about yourself? (No need to be humble here)

DAY #18:

What would your ideal morning routine look like? How can you make this achievable?

DAY #19:

Create a Feel Good playlist in Spotify or your favorite streaming platform. Choose about 10 songs which ALWAYS uplift you and make you feel ready to take on the world. (Don't feel embarrassed by your song choices - you can keep your Playlist private!)

DAY #20:

What actions can you take today to make yourself feel accomplished?

DAY #21:

What beliefs are holding you back from achieving the goals you have? Pen down all these unhelpful beliefs.

Name a teacher, mentor or coach whom you are grateful for. Why are you grateful for 'knowing' him or her? (You don't have to know them personally. You can be grateful to 'know' or be acquainted with Kimberly Springers work, for example)

Terri Terrell

Gratitude for Inner Peace + Positive Feelings

Focusing on the good things in your life will bring happiness and feelings of inner peace. One way to do that is to write 1-3 things you are grateful for, every day.

Being grateful lets you be happy with what you have right now. And it stops you from going out to buy new things or seek new thrills to give you a temporary happiness boost.

Writing a gratitude list is difficult at first, but it gets easier with everyday practice. The key is to write one thing you GENUINELY feel grateful for. Every day will present you with something big or small which brings you a bit - or a lot - of happiness. The trick is to be aware of your blessings and good things which come your way every day.

If you are genuinely happy to have a bright sunny day today, write that down! If you are grateful that your toddler woke up today in a good mood, that counts too. What makes you grateful and happy is entirely personal.

For 21 days, look for little moments or actions every day which bring you happiness. Or, you can create those happy moments yourself!

Have fun!

My 21-Day Gratitude List

DATE	I'm thankful for...
1	
2	
3	
4	
5	
6	
7	
8	
9	
10	
11	
12	
13	
14	
15	
16	

My 21-Day Gratitude List

DATE	I'm thankful for...
17	
18	
19	
20	
21	

"You can't feel fear or anger while feeling gratitude at the same time." - Anthony Robbins

25 Positive Activities for a Good Mood

Keeping your mood as positive as possible means that you can face challenges head on when life throws curveballs at you. Happy people also have more successes at work and relationships. With all these benefits of keeping a positive mindset, it's no wonder that the whole world is obsessed with happiness. Below, I have prepared 25 activities which will bring out feel-good feelings for most of us. As every one of us is unique, you can create your own feel-good activities list in the next page. Have fun!

Cooking + baking	Dancing	Singing to your favourite playlist	Spending time with animals or young children	Taking a warm bath or spending time in water
Meditating for at least 15 mins (check YouTube for guided meditations)	A form of exercise which you enjoy	Reading a fiction novel	Get artistic and create something	Window shopping online + adding items to your cart without checking out
Journaling for at least 20 mins. Google for journal prompts if you need to!	Self care (face masks, hair masks, body scrubs, etc)	Go out in nature	Meeting positive-minded friends	Listening to an uplifting podcast/rewired to love
Decluttering your space	Exploring your life purpose (Hint: it's linked to your joy which is your purpose)	Write your 3 (or more!) skills + talents	Plan your next holiday/outing	Give or donate to someone in need
A 60-min tech detox. (No phones, no laptops, no TV).	Create affirmations which feel good	Surround yourself with beautiful items	Indulge in aromatherapy	Watch anything that makes you laugh

Terri Terrell

My Feel-Good List

In each box below, write down an activity or even item(s) which give you joy. When your vibe is low, or if you feel as though you are in a negative space, look at your own feel-good list and start doing a couple of activities mindfully.

Terri Terrell

Relationships & Positive Thinking

Having a positive mindset requires you to spend time with people who accept you as who you are, and not be judgmental of your choices.

If you feel inspired and energized after meeting someone, it's a sign that you need to meet him or her more often. But if you feel down and drained *every time* after meeting with someone, it's time to cut down the time you 'invest' in this relationship.

In the space below, name 15 people whom you spend the MOST time with. Give each person a **score of 1 - 10** depending on how you feel after meeting or talking to them. A score of 1 means that person makes you feel drained and exhausted whereas '10' means that person makes you feel inspired + in a good mood after meeting or talking to them.

1	Score
2	Score
3	Score
4	Score
5	Score
6	Score
7	Score
8	Score
9	Score
10	Score
11	Score
12	Score
13	Score
14	Score
15	Score

Relationships & Positive Thinking

Is there anything surprising about your list?

Are there people you want to spend less time with? Who are they?

Are there people you want to improve your score with?

What actions can you take to raise the score?

These are the people I want to spend MORE time with:

What characteristics do they have, which make you want to spend more time with them?

How will your life change if you spend more time with people who energize you?

Terri Terrell

Positive Mindset-Shift Cheatsheet

This Cheatsheet will neutralize your negative thoughts when you ask yourself the 6 mindset-shift questions listed below. This will give you more courage + confidence to pursue your goals.

On the left side of this worksheet, write down the negative thoughts that you have daily. Examples will be "I'm not good enough to do (insert activity)…", "I'm not worthy of success", "I don't deserve a luxury lifestyle."

You can neutralize EACH negative thought by asking the 6 questions on the right.

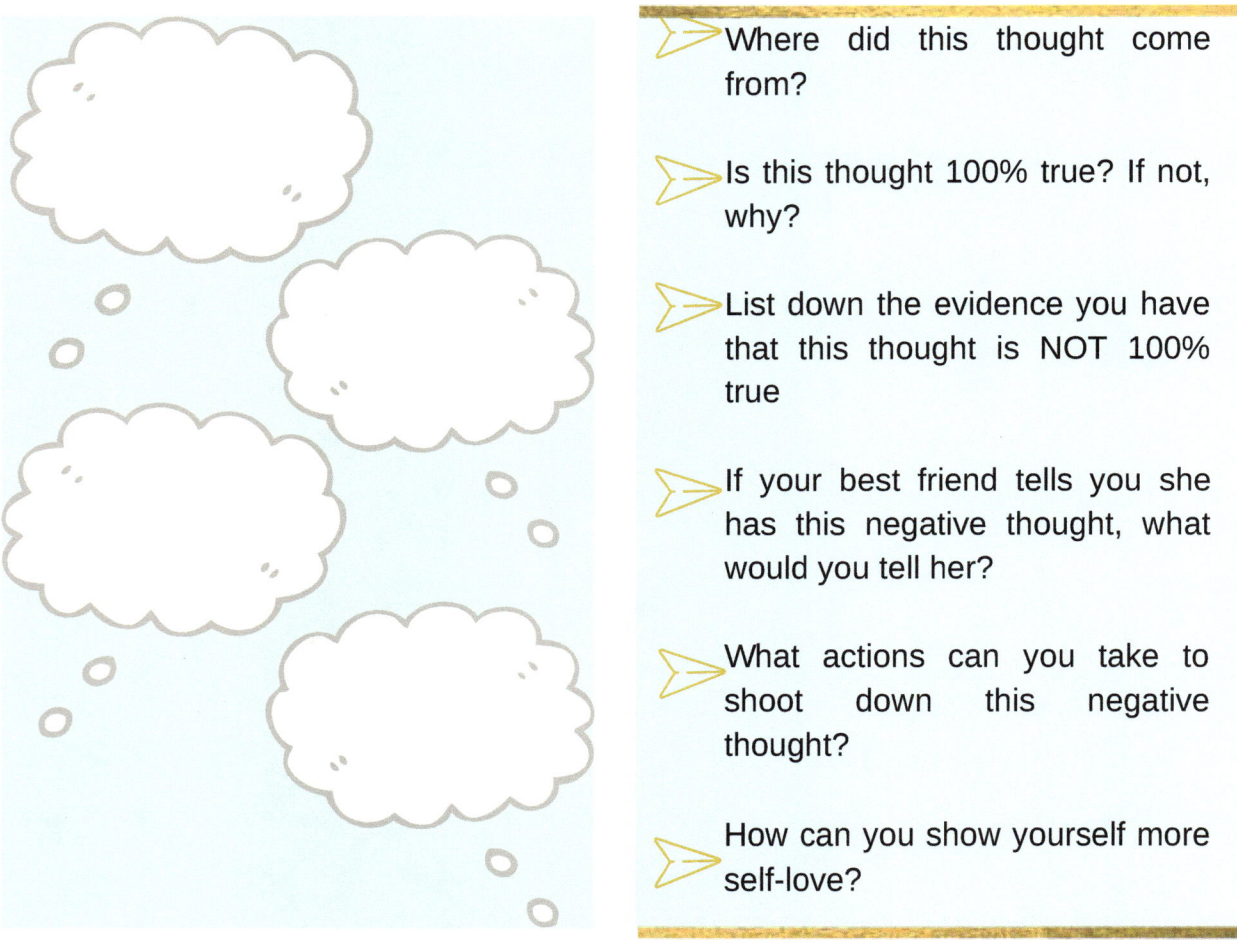

- Where did this thought come from?

- Is this thought 100% true? If not, why?

- List down the evidence you have that this thought is NOT 100% true

- If your best friend tells you she has this negative thought, what would you tell her?

- What actions can you take to shoot down this negative thought?

- How can you show yourself more self-love?

After this, you will be more conscious and even silently questioning your negative thoughts whenever they pop up.

Terri Terrell

Question Your Self-Talk + Feel More Confident

Face your negative self-talk head on with this life-changing tool. You will realize that your self-talk can be irrational and have no basis! This will not instantly boost your self-esteem, but it will make you feel less anxious, less unsure and a little bit more confident of yourself.

How do you complete this worksheet? An example below:

My limiting belief: "I'm not worthy of great success."

Evidence supporting my belief: "I don't have the drive and courage to pursue my goals."

Evidence NOT supporting my belief: "I have great qualifications, relevant experience and the smarts to achieve what I want."

My new balanced belief: "I have the resources + chances to achieve my goals, but have to boost my self-esteem and confidence to achieve them."

My limiting belief	Evidence supporting my belief	Evidence NOT supporting my negative belief	My new balanced belief

Terri Terrell

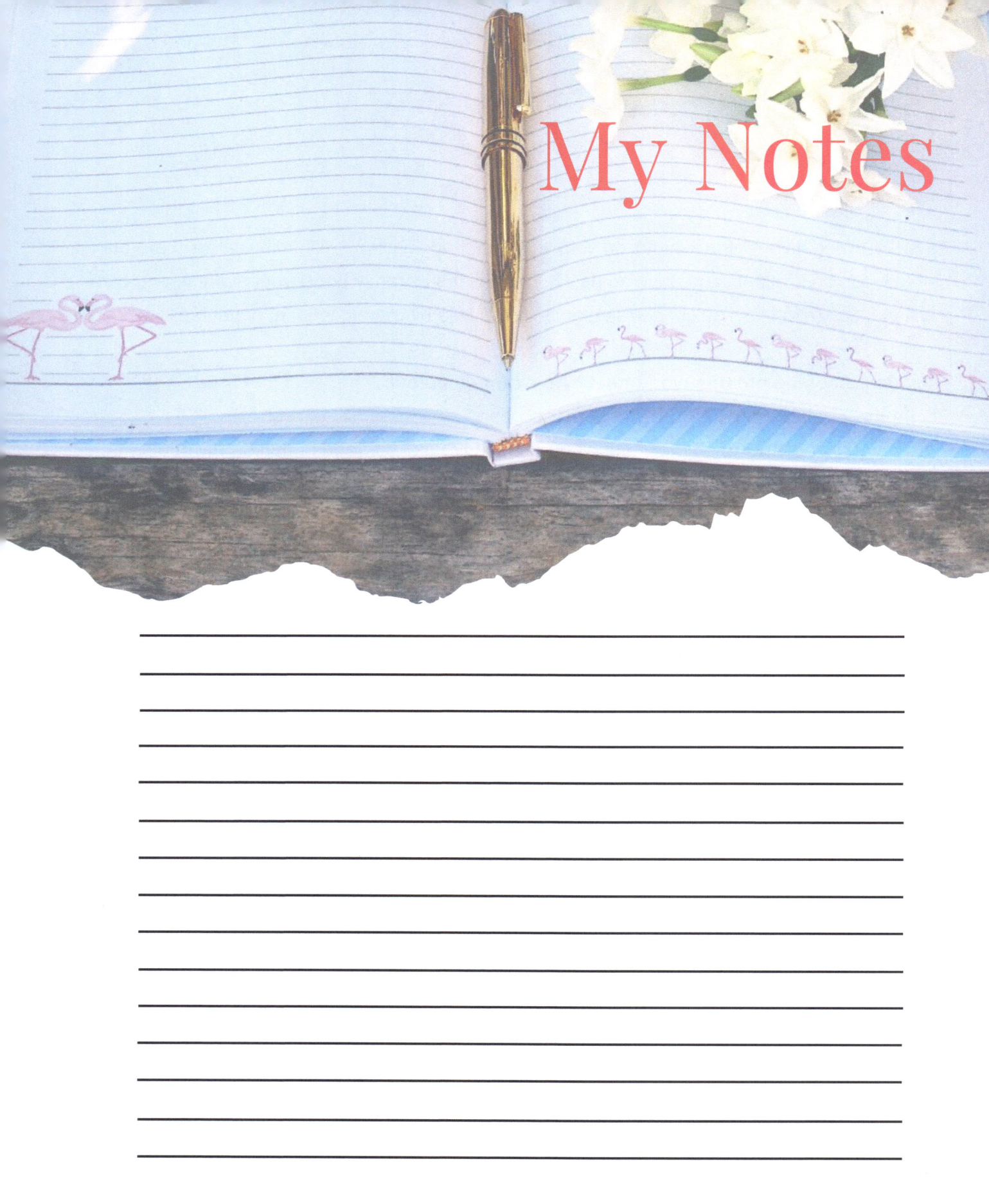

My Notes

My Notes

_____

_____

_____

_____

_____

_____

_____

_____

_____

_____

_____

_____

TerriTerrell

My Notes

_____
_____
_____
_____
_____
_____
_____
_____
_____
_____
_____
_____
_____
_____

TerriTerrell

My Notes

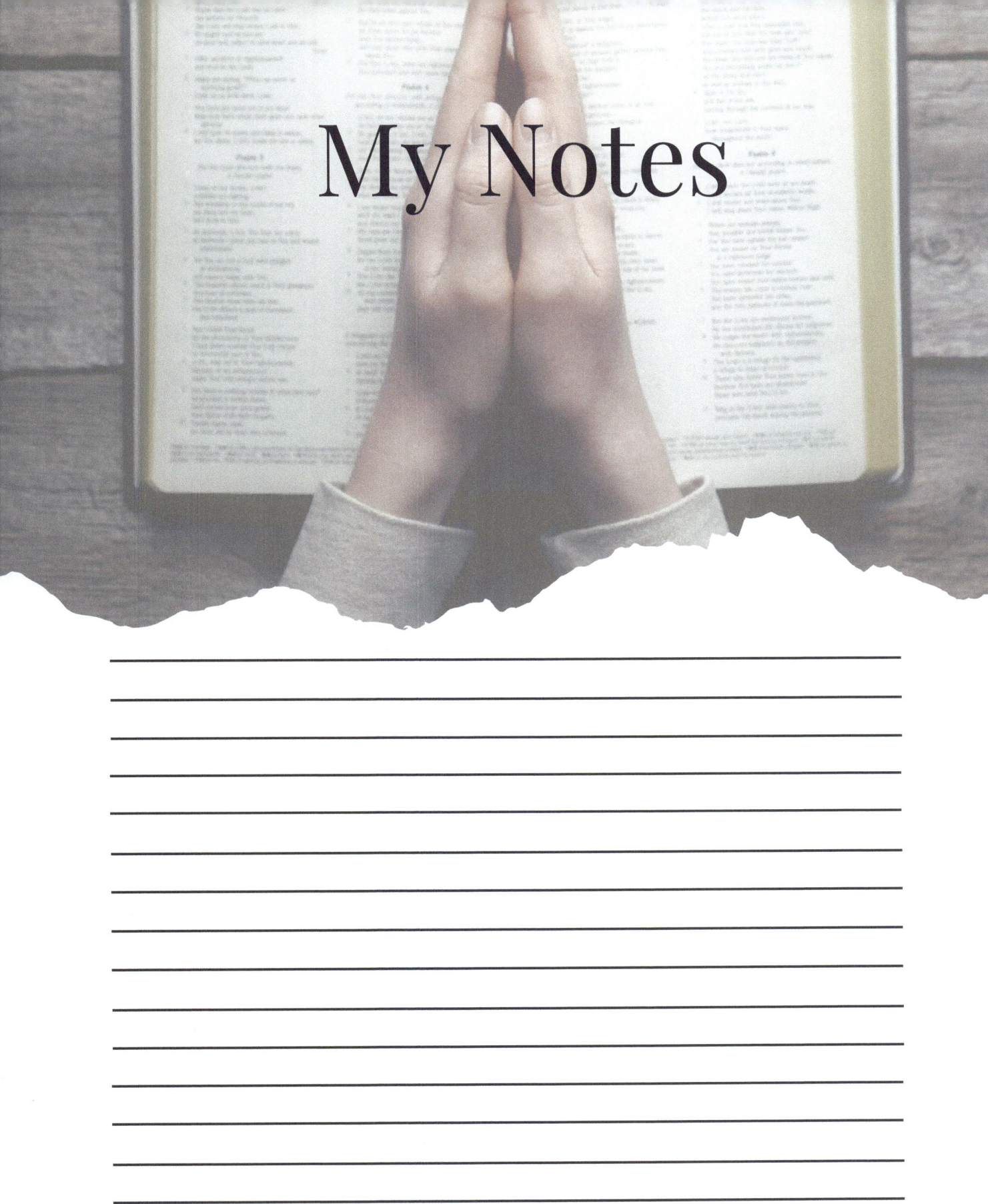

_____
_____
_____
_____
_____
_____
_____
_____
_____
_____
_____
_____
_____

TerriTerrell

My Notes

_____
_____
_____
_____
_____
_____
_____
_____
_____
_____
_____
_____
_____
_____

TerriTerrell

Sign up for my blog updates + follow me on my socials to start your journey to transforming yourself into a confident woman who is brave enough to pursue your goals relentlessly.

BLOG:
Your Confident Mind Matters

FACEBOOK:
@TerriTerrell

INSTAGRAM:
@Terri_Terrell